STICKER ENCYCLOPEDIA

AROUND THE UNITED STATES OF AMERICA

About this book

Author Laura Buller
Editor Sophie Parkes
US Senior Editor Shannon Beatty
Senior Editor Roohi Sehgal
Senior Designer Nidhi Mehra
Project Designer Jaileen Kaur
Assistant Designer Aishwariya Chattoraj
Managing Editor Monica Saigal
Managing Art Editor Romi Chakraborty
Publishing Manager Francesca Young
DTP Designers Sachin Gupta, Vijay Kandwal
Picture Researcher Rituraj Singh
Jacket Coordinator Issy Walsh
Jacket Designers Sonny Flynn, Dheeraj Arora
Jacket Editor Radhika Haswani
Pre-Production Producer Abi Maxwell
Senior Producer Amy Knight
Delhi Team Head Malavika Talukder
Creative Directors Clare Baggaley, Helen Senior
Publishing Director Sarah Larter

First American Edition, 2020
Published in the United States by DK Publishing
1450 Broadway, Suite 801, New York, NY 10018

Copyright © 2020 Dorling Kindersley Limited
DK, a Division of Penguin Random House LLC
20 21 22 23 24 10 9 8 7 6 5 4 3 2 1
001–318861–May/2020

A catalog record for this book
is available from the Library of Congress.
ISBN 978-1-4654-9849-6

DK books are available at special discounts when purchased in bulk for sales
promotions, premiums, fund-raising, or educational use. For details, contact:
DK Publishing Special Markets, 1450 Broadway, Suite 801, New York, NY 10018
SpecialSales@dk.com

Printed and bound in China

A WORLD OF IDEAS:
SEE ALL THERE IS TO KNOW

www.dk.com

DK would like to thank Nimesh Agrawal for additional picture research.

HOW TO USE THIS BOOK

Read the information pages and then search
for the relevant stickers in the back of the book
to fill in the gaps. Use the sticker outlines and
labels to help you.

There are lots of extra stickers that you can use
to decorate the scenes in the back of the book.
It's up to you where you put them all. The most
important thing is to have lots of sticker fun!

The publisher would like to thank the following for their kind permission
to reproduce their photographs:
(Key: a-above; b-below/bottom; c-center; f-far; l-left; r-right; t-top)

123RF.com: Duncan Andison 59ca, 66 (Cherry Blossom), jakobradlgruber 24cl, 50ca, Baiba Opule 62 (lettuce hotdog), 66–67 (lettuce hotdog), 70–71 (lettuce hotdog), Sean Pavone 16clb, 46cb (Street), Solomonjee 5crb, 59bl, Katerina Solovyeva 62 (chowder), 66–67 (chowder), 70–71 (chowder), Sandra van der Steen 2tl, 29cl, 51tr, Ian Yefimkin 62 (banana), 66–67 (banana), 70–71 (banana); **Alamy Stock Photo:** Rolf Adlercreutz 29bl, 51c, All Canada Photos / Jared Hobbs 14c, 43br, 47br, 58fbr, 63 (Owl), Alltravel / Finn Jaschik 30crb, 51cr, Artimages 9cl, 42bc, Backyard Productions 26br, 50br, Ira Berger 59cra, Phillip Bond / © Exploratorium, www.exploratorium.edu 26tr, 51tc, Bill Brooks 25cr, 50c, Engel Ching 18cr, 47tr, ClassicStock / H. ABERNATHY 33cr, 46cb, 54cb, Cloudybright / Carmen K. Sisson 29r, 51br, Yaacov Dagan 35cr, 54br, Ian Dagnall 16cr, 20tr, 46crb, 46bl, dbimages / Allen Brown 12crb, 43bc, Design Pics Inc / Doug Lindstrand 3bc, 20crb, 47c, Terry Donnelly 33b, 55tc, Randy Duchaine 10cr, 43tl, eye35.pix 18b, 47tl, F1online digitale Bildagentur GmbH / Felix Stenson 23cr, 50tr, Don Geyer 7cl, 20–21 (background), 42tl, Jeffrey Isaac Greenberg 5 10–11 (background), Bjorn Grotting 8cra, 42tc (Ferry), imageBROKER / Marc Rasmus 23tl, 50tl, imageBROKER / Michael Szönyi 20clb, 47clb, Raymond Klass 21tl, 47br (Rock), kravka 22cra, 50tc, Chu-Wen Lin 1bl, 8br, 42cr, Melvyn Longhurst 7br, 42tr, Renee McMahon 13cr, 43c, Alice Musbach 12–13 (background), Glenn Nagel 19cr, 47cla, Sean Pavone 17tl, 47ca (car), Pegaz 11cr, 43tc, 59crb, Photo Resource Hawaii / Joe Solem 34cr, 55tl, PixelPod 3bl, 9bl, 42clb, Paul Quayle 27clb, 50bc, robertharding / Michael DeFreitas 6crb, 42tc, Randall Runtsch 32cl, 54cla, Allard Schager 4br, Snapwire / Ai Shieu 4cl,

Solarysys 26cl, 50clb, Mark Summerfield 58bl, SuperStock / Barry Mansell 33cl, 54tr, 66 (Bat), Terry Smith Images 28b, 51ca, 51clb, Bennie Thornton 15cl, 46ca, Derek Trask 25cl, 50cr, Universal Images Group North America LLC / Jumping Rocks 17clb, 47ca, Michael Ventura 10clb, 43cl, Edd Westmacott 13tl, 43bl, Edward Westmacott 27tl, 51tl, 54bl; **Depositphotos Inc:** Alexandra Lande 3tr, 40c, 62 (Karner Blue Butterfly), 66–67 (Karner Blue Butterfly), mihai_tamasila 40; **Dreamstime.com:** Peerasin Aekkathin 40bc, 62–63 (Rabbit), 67 (Rabbit), Albo 62–63 (glove), 67 (glove), 70–71 (glove), Artushfoto 29cb, 50c (harmonica), Rinus Baak 62 (Mule Deer), 67 (Mule Deer), 70–71 (Mule Deer), Gualberto Becerra 3cb, 40clb, 62 (Cloudless Sulphur butterfly), Bhofack2 37bc, 55br, 58cl, 66–67 (Beans), Biolifepics 22clb, 47bl, Steve Byland 62 (Scrub-Jay), 67 (Scrub-Jay), 70–71 (Scrub-Jay), Cafebeanz Company 12tr, 42cra, 43clb, Howard Cheek 40br, 62–63 (White-tailed Deer), 66 (White-tailed Deer), 70–71 (White-tailed Deer), Czalewski 28c, 51cla, Svetlana Day 18cl, 47cr, James Deboer 59clb, 66–67 (Turtle), 70–71 (Turtle), Erix2005 25b, 50cb, F11photo 28cr, 46tr, 50bl, Sue Feldberg 62 (Gray Squirrel), 66 (Gray Squirrel), 70–71 (Gray Squirrel), Iakov Filimonov 58br, 62–63 (Jaguar), 66 (Jaguar), 70–71 (Jaguar), Anton Gorbachev 36bc, 55cb, Diego Grandi 9crb, 17tr, 42crb, 46clb (Crosswalk), Haveseen 14bl, 46tc, Heromen30 62 (Basketball), 66 (Basketball), 70–71 (Basketball), Anton Ignatenco 70–71 (Apple), Irusik48 62–63 (Hamburger), 66–67 (Hamburger), 70–71 (Hamburger), Isselee 1bc, 58crb (panda), 62–63 (panda), 67 (Bison), 62–63 (panda), 67 (Panda), 70–71 (Bison), Jenifoto406 35tl, 54crb, Ritu Jethani 12cl, 43cr, Jgorzynik 22crb, 47cb, Kcmatt 62 (rattlesnake), 66 (rattlesnake), 70–71 (rattlesnake), Kiselevkirill 40cb, 62 (Red Squirrel), Lev Kropotov 51cb, 58fcrb (sacura tree), 59tl, 59br, 63 (Sacura tree), 67 (Sacura tree), Ld1976d 63 (Apple pie), Lequint 26–27 (background), Luckyphotographer 14r, 17br, 21cra, 23tr, 46tl, 46br, 47cra, 50cla, Lunamarina 30–31 (background), Marysmn 34–35 (background), Supitcha Mcadam 15cr, 46clb, Sirinarth Mekvorawuth 36–37, Olga Mendenhall 19b, 46c, 47cl, Oleksandra Naumenko 36c, 55cr, 63 (Turkey), 67 (Turkey), Ncristian 1br, 40cb (Violet Saintpaulias), 62–63 (African violets), 66–67 (African violets), Nevinates 62 (Blueberries), 66–67 (Blueberries), 70–71 (Blueberries), Paulacobleigh 34cl, 47bc, 54bc, 55tr, 58crb, 59bc, 63 (Fireworks), Sean Pavone 7tl, 22–23 (background), 31clb, 42ca, 51bl, 55cra, Denis Pepin 63 (American Football), Pictureguy66 40cla (Blue Jay), 62 (Blue Jay), Pigprox 5tl, Pioneer111 37cl, 55cl, 63 (Candlestick), 66–67 (Candlestick), Beatrice Preve 5bl, Paul Reeves 47bc (Wood Thrush), 58fcrb, 59cla, 59br, 62 (Wood Thrush), 66–67 (Bird on branch), 66–67 (Wood Thrush), 70–71 (Wood Thrush), Pongpon Rinthaisong 5tr, Rkpimages 1crb, 40ca, 62–63 (Bald Eagle), 67 (Bald Eagle), Sgoodwin4813 30tr, 54cra, Sandra Sims 40clb (Mountain Laurel), 62 (Mountain Laurel), 66–67 (Mountain Laurel), Smileus 36–37 (Leaves), 55 (leaves), 58 (leaves), 63 (Leaves), 66–67 (Leaves), Roman Stetsyk 31crb, 54tl, Jack Tade 62 (Lincoln), Tupungato 6tr, 42c, Gale Verhague 62 (American Goldfinch), 66–67 (American Goldfinch), 70–71 (American Goldfinch), Birute Vijeikiene 62 (Red-eared slider), 66–67 (Red-eared slider), 70–71 (Red-eared slider), Whitestorm 43clb, 58tl, 63 (Pumpkin pie), 67 (Pumpkin pie), Yvdavyd 62–63 (Blackberries), 67 (Blackberries), 70–71 (Blackberries), Iwona Ziomek 37crb, 58tc, 63 (Vase), 67 (Vase); **Getty Images:** 500px / Melissa James 21br, 43cb (Spoonbill), 47crb, AFP / Mark Ralston 34tr, 54cr, Jose Azel 8clb, 42cb, The Boston Globe / Dina Rudick 13br, 43cb, Moment / Jeff R Clow 31tl, 54tc, Corbis Documentary / © James P. Blair / Corbis / VCG 11tr, 42br, DigitalVision / Matteo Colombo 6–7 (background), The Image Bank / Hisham Ibrahim 3br, 35bl, 54clb, Moment / Image by Michael Rickard 30clb, 51bc, 63 (Horse), Stockbyte / Michele Falzone 15b, 46cra, The Washington Post / Xiaomei Chen 27cb, 51tc (boy); **iStockphoto.com:** Camrocker 23clb, 50cra, f11photo 6clb, 42cl, JPecha 59tr, OksanaKiian 62–63 (Macaroni), 66–67 (Macaroni), Sean Pavone 16–17 (background), 24b, 50crb, pilgrims49 32b, 54cl, pjohnson1 70–71 (Hotdog Sausage), Jennifer_Sharp 24cr, 50cl, Supercaliphotolistic 40cla, 62 (Meadowlark); **NASA:** 11tl, 43ca; **The Metropolitan Museum of Art:** Gift of John D. Rockefeller Jr., 1932 11bl, 43tr

Cover images: *Front and Back:* **Dreamstime.com:** Rozbyshaka; *Front:* **Alamy Stock Photo:** Ron Buskirk cra, David Cabrera Navarro crb, James Pintar, Andrew Unangst br; **Dreamstime.com:** Jerryway cb, Luciano Mortula l, Pixelpodllc c; *Back:* **123RF.com:** Sandra van der Steen crb; **Alamy Stock Photo:** eye35.pix tc, F1online digitale Bildagentur GmbH / Felix Stenson cr, James Pintar c/ (Fireworks); **Dreamstime.com:** Tupungato cb; **Getty Images:** Melissa James / 500px clb

All other images © Dorling Kindersley
For further information see: www.dkimages.com

Contents

Discover the United States!

Take a trip around the United States! There is so much to discover across the 50 states. Here are some of the country's most famous landmarks.

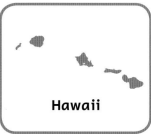

Alaska

Hawaii

Washington

Oregon

Montana

North Dakota

Idaho

South Dakota

Wyoming

Nebraska

Nevada

California

Utah

Colorado

Kansas

Arizona

Oklahoma

New Mexico

Texas

The Golden Gate Bridge, San Francisco

This beautiful structure in California is thought to be the most photographed bridge in the world. Discover more on page 18.

Santa Monica Pier, California

Take a beach vacation in Santa Monica, and visit the pier for roller coasters and its famous ferris wheel! Find it on page 30.

Chicago River, Chicago

Made up of lots of different rivers and canals, the Chicago River is an amazing 156 miles (251 km) long!

Statue of Liberty, New York

Holding her golden torch high over New York City, the Statue of Liberty is an American icon. Find out more on page 8.

Minnesota

Wisconsin

Michigan

Iowa

Illinois

Indiana

Ohio

Missouri

Kentucky

Arkansas

Tennessee

Mississippi

Alabama

Louisiana

Georgia

Florida

Vermont

Maine

New Hampshire

New York

Rhode Island

Massachusetts

Connecticut

Pennsylvania

New Jersey

Maryland

Delaware

West Virginia

Virginia

North Carolina

South Carolina

The White House, Washington, D.C.

Welcome to the home of the President of the United States! Every president since John Adams in 1800 (who was the second president) has lived here.

Key West, Florida

This island city lies on the southern tip of the United States. It's only about 90 miles (145 km) from Cuba, which is in the Caribbean.

Historical landmarks

Explore the places where history was made! There are around 2,600 official National Historic Landmarks in the United States, and countless other amazing places to see.

US Capitol Building, Washington, D.C.

The United States Congress meet here to make and shape laws. Underneath the huge building are underground tunnels and a private subway system.

Gateway Arch, St. Louis

A tram whisks visitors to the top of this 63-story concrete and steel structure. The arch celebrates all the pioneers who helped people to settle in the American west.

Fort Sumter, Charleston

Kaboom! In 1861, cannons from this Confederate Army fort on an island off Charleston pounded the Union Army. This was the first battle of the American Civil War.

The Alamo, San Antonio

In 1836, the Republic of Texas and Mexico were fighting over control of Texan lands. The Mexicans won a 13-day battle at the Alamo, a walled fortress.

FACT!

The foundations for Seattle's Space Needle are so deep that it took 467 cement trucks a whole day to fill them.

Space Needle, Seattle

This icon was built for the 1962 World's Fair in Seattle. There are glass-walled observation decks, as well as the world's only rotating glass floor, which provide a spectacular view of the city.

Old North Church, Boston

On the eve of the Revolutionary War, two lanterns were hung in the steeple of this church to signal that the British Army was invading Boston on land.

Statue of Liberty

With her torch lighting a welcome to America, the Statue of Liberty is an icon. The huge copper statue was a gift from France to the United States, to celebrate its 100th birthday.

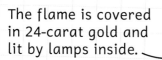
The flame is covered in 24-carat gold and lit by lamps inside.

Liberty Island
Ferries cross the Hudson River in Manhattan to reach the statue and a museum.

Visitors climb 354 steps to reach the crown for a spectacular view.

Happy Birthday, America!
To celebrate Independence Day on the Fourth of July, a firework display lights up the sky around Lady Liberty.

Liberty Bell

The most famous bell in America, the Liberty Bell hangs in Philadelphia. It was rung to mark special events. However, it doesn't ring anymore—around 1846, the bell cracked.

FACT FILE

Location: Pennsylvania
Height: 3 ft (1 m)
Opened: 1752
Fun fact: During the Revolutionary War, the bell was hidden so British troops didn't steal it to make cannons.

The Declaration of Independence
In 1776, American patriots signed a document to cut their ties with Great Britain. It is thought that the bell was rung when the Declaration was first read out.

Independence Hall
The bell hangs here, where the Declaration of Independence and Constitution were signed.

Ringing for liberty
The huge crack means the bell cannot ring now, but you can download an app to hear what it sounded like.

Museums and memorials

There are thousands of museums across America. There, you can discover everything from world-famous works of art, priceless artifacts, and valuable books, to salt-and-pepper shakers, bad art, and UFOs.

National Museum of African American History and Culture, Washington, D.C.
This museum opened in 2016 and contains more than 30,000 artifacts. Its design is based on traditional African art—its outside is wrapped in woven metalwork.

Cleveland Museum of Art, Ohio
The collection at this free museum spans about 6,000 years. It contains almost 45,000 amazing objects from all over the world.

Kennedy Space Center Visitor Complex, Florida

It's a blast visiting this complex dedicated to space exploration. There are rockets from every space program and artifacts that tell the exciting story of NASA.

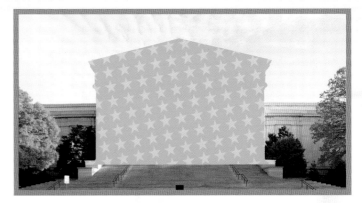

National Gallery of Art, Washington, D.C.

A collection of about 141,000 paintings, drawings, photographs, sculptures, and more tells the story of art to visitors here.

DID YOU KNOW?

The National Museum of Natural History in Washington, D.C. is the most visited museum in the United States.

Martin Luther King, Jr. National Historic Site, Georgia

Hear the story of this inspirational figure in the Civil Rights Movement at the places in Atlanta where he was born, lived, and worked.

Metropolitan Museum of Art, New York

Here, discover the famous collection of American art, old objects from across the world (such as this winged lion from ancient Iraq), and some 2,500 of Europe's finest paintings.

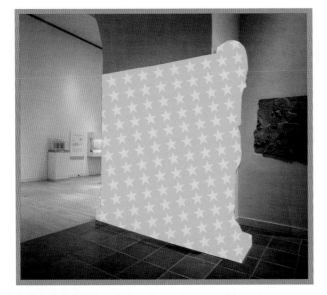

Park life

Want to escape the hustle and bustle of the city, kick a ball around with friends, or enjoy a picnic in the sun? Head to one of the United States' public parks.

Lincoln Park, Chicago

The largest public park in Chicago, Lincoln Park is home to more than 1,000 incredible animals, thanks to its famous zoo which has everything from lions to lemurs. Best of all, it's free, so visitors can go wild!

Hermann Park, Houston

This park has beautiful gardens, a lake for paddle boating, and a train. Its Pioneer Obelisk honors those who founded the Texan city.

Griffith Park, Los Angeles

Located high on a hill, this park is full of riding and hiking trails. Its Observatory has amazing views of the city and the stars in the sky.

Central Park, New York

Visit a mini castle, go ice skating, or hike through the trees, right in the center of New York City! Central Park was founded in 1853.

Forest Park, St. Louis

This beautiful park is home to three museums, a zoo, and a science center. Its Nathan Frank Memorial bandstand is a popular landmark.

DID YOU KNOW?

Depending on where you are, you might find bats, opossums, foxes, hawks, owls, or turtles sharing a park with you!

Boston Common, Boston

America's oldest city park, Boston Common, welcomes everyone to stroll, play, or smile at its famous duckling statues. You can see real ducklings, too!

Redwood National and State Parks

California's 1,000 year-old redwood trees are the tallest living things on Earth. They are home to a range of wild animals, from spotted owls to giant banana slugs.

FACT FILE

Location: California
Area: 132,000 acres (534,000 sq km)
Climate: Dry summers, mild and wet winters
Fun fact: Thick bark protects the trees from fire and disease.

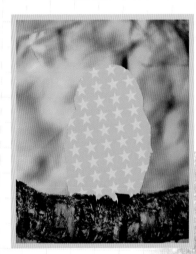

Northern spotted owl

Tunnel Log in Sequoia National Park
Visitors can drive a car through a tunnel cut in this 2,000-year-old fallen tree.

Grand Canyon

Over about 6 million years, the Colorado River carved this incredible canyon through the red rock of Arizona. Today, more than 6 million visitors a year visit to marvel at its size.

FACT FILE

Location: Arizona
Area: 1,902 sq miles (4,926 sq km)
Climate: Hot and dry summers, cold winters
Fun fact: There are about 1,000 caves tucked inside the canyon walls.

Desert View Watchtower
Perched on the edge of the canyon, this tower gives visitors a spectacular view of the canyon.

Visitors climb 85 stairs to reach the tower.

Skywalk
Feeling brave? Step onto the skywalk, a glass platform 4,000 ft (1,219 m) above the canyon floor. It's strong enough to hold 70 fully loaded jet planes.

People have lived in the canyon for more than 12,000 years.

Famous streets

Almost every town in the United States, no matter how large or small, has a Main Street. Yet some streets have become famous around the world, and are tourist attractions in their own right.

Acorn Street, Boston
This street in Boston's Beacon Hill is paved with cobblestones. The round stones, each one different, make a beautiful (but bumpy) street.

French Quarter, New Orleans
The St. Louis Cathedral is in the French Quarter, the oldest neighborhood in New Orleans.

Hollywood Boulevard, Los Angeles

Look down at the stars on Hollywood Boulevard! The sidewalks are covered with names of famous stars from movies and television.

Chicago Riverwalk, Chicago

Once a shipping channel, the Chicago Riverwalk is a cool walkway that spans 1¼ miles (2 km) along the Chicago River.

Pennsylvania Avenue, Washington, D.C.

This historic street in the nation's capital connects the US Capitol with the country's most famous address, 1600 Pennsylvania Avenue—the White House!

Castro Street, San Francisco

Rainbow flags and rainbow-striped crosswalks welcome visitors to the Castro District. The vibrant neighborhood is the historical center of the LGBTQ movement in the city.

FACT!

The longest street in America may be Colfax Avenue in Denver, Colorado, at 50 miles (80 km) long.

The Golden Gate Bridge

Connecting San Francisco to the north of California, the Golden Gate Bridge is one of the most beautiful feats of engineering in the world.

Fort Point
This fort at the southern base of the bridge helped to defend the city after the Gold Rush through to World War II.

Front view of bridge
About 112,000 vehicles cross the bridge every day.

Two towers 746 ft (227 m) tall support the bridge's cables.

Cables are made of more than sixty bundles of steel wire twisted together.

Mount Rushmore

The faces of four presidents are carved into Mount Rushmore in South Dakota. The majestic, mile-high monument celebrates the early history of the United States in a unique way.

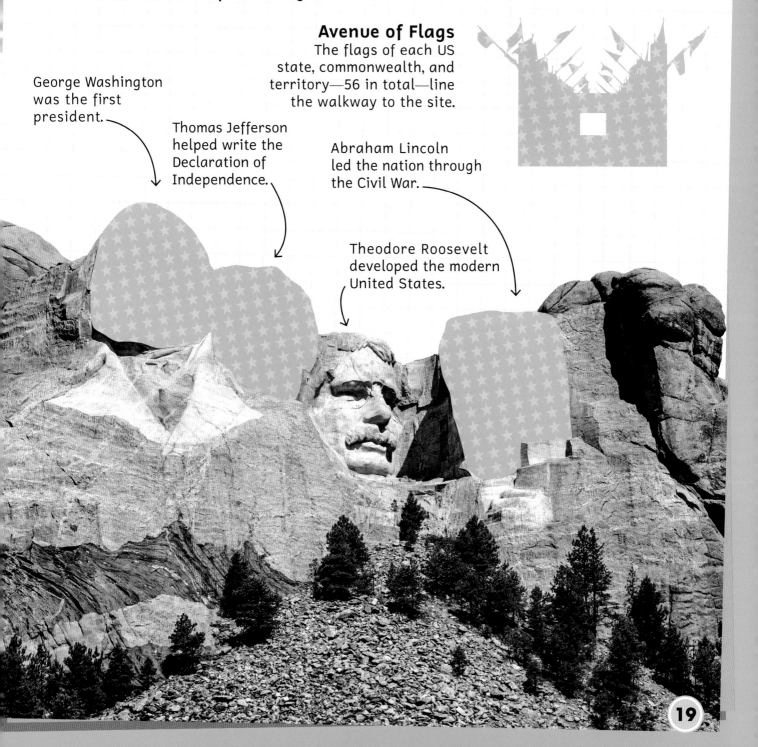

Avenue of Flags
The flags of each US state, commonwealth, and territory—56 in total—line the walkway to the site.

George Washington was the first president.

Thomas Jefferson helped write the Declaration of Independence.

Abraham Lincoln led the nation through the Civil War.

Theodore Roosevelt developed the modern United States.

National parks

From the snowy peaks of Alaska to the sunny Florida shores, the United States' 61 incredible national parks invite visitors to enjoy nature. Whether visitors want to hike, camp, take in the scenery, or spot wildlife, they will find plenty to explore.

Yosemite National Park, California
This park in the High Sierra mountain range is famous for its massive valleys and waterfalls. Climbers scale its huge mountains, such as Half Dome, shown here.

Olympic National Park, Washington, D.C.
With miles of rugged coastline as well as forests and glacier-topped mountain peaks, this park has a range of environments suitable for all sorts of wildlife, such as this mountain-loving marmot.

Denali National Park, Alaska
North America's tallest mountain, 20,310 ft (6,190 m) can be found in this park, as well as all kinds of wild animals, from grizzly bears to these curly-horned Dall's sheep.

DID YOU KNOW?
There are around 85 million acres of national parkland in the US. That's one long hike!

Voyageurs National Park, Minnesota

More than 40 percent of this river and lake-filled park is water. Even more amazingly, there are ancient volcanic rocks here visitors can see and touch that are half as old as the Earth itself!

Yellowstone National Park, Wyoming

It sits on top of a super volcano, boiling hot geysers shoot into the sky, and hot springs in wild colors bubble. However, Yellowstone, the oldest national park, gets millions of visitors a year.

FACT!

California is the state with the most national parks—it has nine. Alaska is in second place with eight.

Everglades National Park, Florida

Many rare animals live in this tropical wilderness, from endangered animals like the Florida panther and the manatee, to a few hundred of these roseate spoonbills.

...and more parks!

The National Park system protects and preserves more than 84 million acres of land. Yet it's not all wilderness—there are historical sites, monuments, battlefields, seashores, parkways, and lakeshores.

DID YOU KNOW?

You'll find a former prison (Alcatraz) at the Golden Gate National Recreation Area in California.

Mesa Verde National Park, Colorado

More than 700 years ago, the Pueblo people lived in incredible stone villages built into canyon walls. They farmed on the cliffs above.

Acadia National Park, Maine

From beaches to the tallest mountain on the Atlantic Coast, this park is home to lots of different plant species and animals, including the odd moose!

Grand Teton National Park, Wyoming

The wildlife at this park is really wild! Among the snowy peaks and valleys, visitors may encounter bison, elk, bears, and bighorn sheep.

Carlsbad Caverns National Park, New Mexico

This underground cave system is filled with incredible mineral formations called speleothems. More than 300,000 bats fill the caves, too.

Arches National Park, Utah

More than 2,000 natural sandstone arches of all sizes dot the landscape of this amazing natural wonder. Spot spikes, spires, and plenty more!

Joshua Tree National Park, California

The twisty branches and spiky leaves of the Joshua tree are an amazing sight. The trees shelter dozens of desert-dwelling animals.

Shenandoah National Park, Virginia

There are 500 miles (805 km) of hiking trails in this mountainous park. Cruise along Skyline Drive for views of the valleys, and deer and black bears, too.

FACT!

Great Smoky Mountains National Park in Tennessee is the most visited park in the United States.

Hoover Dam

The mighty Hoover Dam uses the flow of water from the Colorado River to supply power for four states. It also delivers water to homes—a drink from a tap in Los Angeles may come from here!

FACT FILE

Location: Nevada-Arizona border
Height: 726 ft (221 m)
Built: 1931–36
Fun fact: All the concrete in the dam could build a sidewalk around the Earth at the Equator.

Intake towers
The water to power the dam and make electricity flows in through these huge towers.

Power up!
All that water makes turbines (giant blades) inside the dam spin. Generators turn the water power into electricity.

Lake Mead is the reservoir created by the dam. It is America's largest reservoir.

Niagara Falls

The sheer amount of fast-moving water pouring over Niagara Falls makes them a sight to see. Around 700,000 gallons of water (28 million liters) crash down every second.

Under the spray
Brave tourists who want to get up close to the Falls can put on raincoats and take boats right into the spray.

Icy Falls
In winter, the Falls freeze in places.

Three different falls, the American and Bridal Veil (above) and the Horseshoe Falls (right), make up the Niagara Falls.

Just for kids

Imagine a museum where you can learn, play, and touch things, too! There are cool attractions all over the United States. Meet animals past and present, discover how science works, and have a treetop adventure.

Exploratorium, San Francisco
In 1969, this museum became the first to collect items to help curious kids learn about science and the world by doing and touching, not just looking!

American Museum of National History, New York
The world's largest natural history museum is packed with more than 40 galleries. You can dig up a dinosaur or soar through the stars at the Hayden Planetarium.

FACT!
Cedar Point, Ohio is the roller coaster capital of America, with 16 different thrill rides.

San Diego Safari Park, San Diego
Soar over this safari park in a hot air balloon, and see how many animals you can spot, including lions, tigers, and more!

Bronx Zoo, New York

More than 6,000 animals from 700 species make their home in this urban zoo, one of the largest in the United States. There is even a zoo animal hospital!

Monterey Bay Aquarium, Monterey

Explore around 35,000 ocean creatures on a visit to this spectacular aquarium. The aquarium works to protect ocean life, too.

Sandy Spring Adventure Park, Maryland

Challenge yourself at the biggest aerial forest adventure park in North America. Climb, zipline, and swing between platforms high in the trees.

Trail of Tears

In 1830, the US government passed a law allowing them to force indigenous people to move from the Southeast to new lands in Oklahoma. Today, the difficult route the indigenous people took is a National Historic Trail.

FACT FILE

Location: Southeastern United States
Started in: 1838–1839
Main participants: Cherokee, Creek, Chickasaw, Choctaw
Fun fact: Some traveled by horse and wagon, but many made the journey on foot.

Cherokee basket
Although the indigenous people, including the Cherokee nation, fought back through the courts, they were forced to move. They were given no time to collect their belongings.

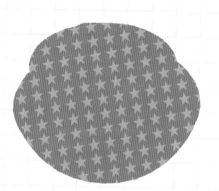

Mississippi River
Some people traveled to the new lands by steamboat on the Mississippi River.

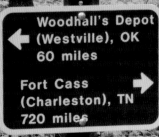

Woodhall's Depot
(Westville), OK
← 60 miles

Fort Cass
(Charleston), TN
720 miles →

Mississippi Blues Trail

Explore Mississippi, the birthplace of the blues, and visit the places where the music was made. Sites all over the state tell the stories of the musicians and the music they played.

Highway 61 is known as the "Blues Highway."

Legend says musician Robert Johnson traded his soul to the devil to play blues guitar.

Saxophone

Harmonica

Museums along the trail
Some of the most fascinating stops along the trail are blues museums, collections of cool blues memorabilia.

Devil's Crossroads

Hit the beach!

Want to build the biggest sandcastle or catch a wild wave? Head to one of the United States' coastal or island beaches. There is plenty of natural beauty, from rocky sea stacks to tide pools, and lots of fun, too.

Cape Hatteras National Seashore, North Carolina

Want to climb the tallest brick lighthouse in North America? Cape Hatteras Light, on the shores of the Outer Banks, is 257 steps high—the same as a 12-story building!

Assateague Island, Maryland and Virginia

Seahorses? Not quite, but herds of wild horses make their home on this coastal island. More than 300 horses roam across the beaches and forests.

Santa Monica Beach, California

This beach is huge—245 acres in total! Visitors can surf the waves, and then enjoy a roller coaster ride at the amusement park on Santa Monica Pier afterward.

Cannon Beach, Oregon

Soaring seabirds and colorful puffins are among the many animals who live near Haystack Rock on Cannon Beach, a landmark formed millions of years ago on the Oregon shore.

Miami Beach, Florida

This island beach on the Atlantic coast is famous for its Art Deco architecture. Even its 36 lifeguard stations are colorful and bright, and each one is unique.

Myrtle Beach, South Carolina

With 60 miles (97 km) of sandy beaches, this resort is a family favorite. An old-fashioned boardwalk and the highest ferris wheel on the East Coast add to the fun.

Pikes Peak

Known as "America's Mountain," Pikes Peak rises high above the Rocky Mountains. Some of its trees are more than 2,000 years old. Elk, mountain lions, and black bears live near the summit.

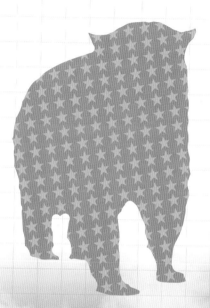

Black bear

World's highest cog train
Opened in 1891, the cog railway lifts visitors to the top of Pikes Peak.

Buffalo National River

Flowing through the Ozark Mountains, the Buffalo River is the first river to join the National Parks. 250 species of birds, 55 of mammals, and 59 of fish live here.

FACT FILE

Location: Arkansas
Length: 135 miles (217 km)
Climate: Hot summers, mild winters
Fun fact: There are more than 500 caves in the national park, and springs that seem to disappear!

Big-eared bat

Picturesque waterfalls
Hikers trek through the park to explore its amazing waterfalls. In spring, beautiful wildflowers bloom.

Festivals and celebrations

It's time to celebrate! There are ten official holidays every year in the United States, but people celebrate all sorts of occasions. Some of these special days are global, but others are strictly all-American.

Memorial Day
Every year on the last Monday in May, we remember the men and women who died serving the United States Armed Forces. People place flags on the graves of the fallen.

Fourth of July
Independence Day celebrates the signing of the Declaration of Independence on July 4, 1776. Fireworks light up the night sky and people gather for fun.

Aloha Festival
This month-long festival celebrates the heritage of the state of Hawaii. There is traditional music and dancing, and colorful, flower-filled parades fill the streets.

DID YOU KNOW?
Nearly two billion striped candy canes are made for the Christmas holiday.

Thanksgiving

On the fourth Thursday in November, America celebrates Thanksgiving. This feast celebrates a gathering of the English Pilgrims and the Wampanoag people after a good harvest.

St. Patrick's Day

Each year on March 17, America seems to turn green. People wear green clothes, drink green milkshakes, and the city of Chicago even dyes its river green to celebrate Irish heritage.

Halloween

BOO! People celebrate Halloween on October 31. They carve scary faces into pumpkins, dress up in amazing costumes, and trick-or-treat through the streets for candy.

Thanksgiving

Use the stickers in the book to fill up this page. You might find the items listed below on the dinner table at Thanksgiving.

- ☐ Turkey
- ☐ Pumpkin pie
- ☐ Autumn flowers
- ☐ Mashed potatoes
- ☐ Green beans
- ☐ Cranberry sauce
- ☐ Candlestick
- ☐ Stuffing
- ☐ Autumn leaves

Washington, D.C.

CHECKLIST

Use the stickers in the book to fill up this page. You might find the items below in Washington, D.C., the capital of the United States.

- ☐ Supreme Court
- ☐ Smithsonian Museum
- ☐ Eastern box turtle
- ☐ Lincoln Memorial
- ☐ Eastern gray squirrel
- ☐ Wood thrush
- ☐ The White House
- ☐ Cherry tree in blossom
- ☐ Nationals Park
- ☐ Martin Luther King, Jr. National Historic Site

Into the woods

CHECKLIST

Use the stickers in the book to fill up this page. You might find the items listed below in different forests across the United States.

- [ ] Bald eagle
- [ ] Meadowlark
- [ ] Blue jay
- [ ] Butterflies
- [ ] Red squirrel
- [ ] White-tailed deer
- [ ] Violet flowers
- [ ] Mountain laurel flowers
- [ ] Rabbit

Space Needle,
Seattle

Fort Sumter,
Charleston

The Alamo,
San Antonio

Liberty Island

Old North
Church, Boston

U.S. Capitol
Building,
Washington, D.C.

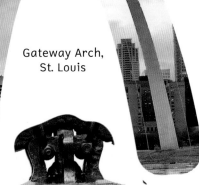

Gateway Arch,
St. Louis

Statue of
Liberty

Independence
Hall

Liberty Bell

Happy Birthday,
America!

The Declaration
of Independence

National Gallery of Art, Washington, D.C.

Metropolitan Museum of Art, New York

Martin Luther King, Jr. National Historic Site, Georgia

Cleveland Museum of Art, Ohio

Kennedy Space Center Visitor Complex, Florida

National Museum of African American History and Culture, Washington, D.C.

Forest Park, St. Louis

Lincoln Park, Chicago

Hermann Park, Houston

Boston Common, Boston

Central Park, New York

Griffith Park, Los Angeles

Northern spotted owl

Tunnel Log in Sequoia National Park

Skywalk

Abraham
Lincoln

Desert View
Watchtower

Grand
Canyon

Redwood
National
and State
Parks

French Quarter,
New Orleans

Acorn Street,
Boston

Castro Street, San Francisco

Yellowstone
National Park,
Wyoming

Yosemite National
Park, California

The Golden Gate Bridge

Front view of bridge

Avenue of Flags

Chicago Riverwalk, Chicago

Pennsylvania Avenue, Washington, D.C.

Hollywood Boulevard, Los Angeles

Fort Point

George Washington

Thomas Jefferson

Denali National Park, Alaska

Olympic National Park, Washington, D.C.

Everglades National Park, Florida

Acadia National Park, Maine

Grand Teton National Park, Wyoming

Voyageurs National Park, Minnesota

Carlsbad Caverns
National Park,
New Mexico

Mesa Verde National Park,
Colorado

Joshua Tree National
Park, California

Intake
towers

Shenandoah National
Park, Virginia

Arches National Park, Utah

Under the
spray

Power up!

Harmonica

Icy Falls

Niagara
Falls

Hoover
Dam

American
Museum of
National History,
New York

Monterey Bay
Aquarium, Monterey

Mississippi
River

San Diego Safari
Park, San Diego

Bronx Zoo,
New York

Exploratorium,
San Francisco

Sandy Spring Adventure
Park, Maryland

Saxophone

Cherokee basket

Trail of
Tears

Museums
along
the trail

Santa Monica
Beach, California

Trail of
Tears

TRAIL OF TEARS

NATIONAL HISTORIC TRAIL

Original Route

Devil's
Crossroads

Assateague Island,
Maryland and
Virginia

Myrtle
Beach,
South
Carolina

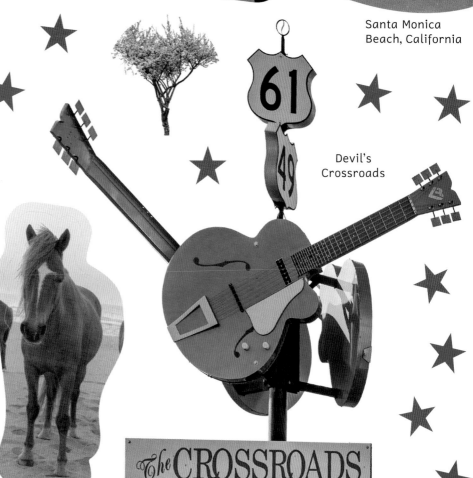

The CROSSROADS

Miami Beach, Florida

Cannon Beach, Oregon

Big-eared bat

Black bear

World's highest cog train

Cape Hatteras National Seashore, North Carolina

Pikes Peak

Memorial Day

Picturesque waterfalls

Thanksgiving

Happy Thanksgiving

Halloween

Fourth of July

St. Patrick's Day

Aloha Festival

Buffalo National River

Stickers for the Thanksgiving scene on pages 36-37

Turkey

Candlestick

Mashed potatoes

Stuffing

Autumn leaves

Pumpkin pie

Autumn flowers

Green beans

Cranberry sauce

Autumn leaves

Stickers for the Washington, D.C. scene on pages 38-39

Smithsonian Museum

Cherry tree
in blossom

Supreme Court

Wood thrush

Eastern gray squirrel

Nationals Park

Martin Luther
King, Jr. National
Historic Site

Eastern box turtle

The White House

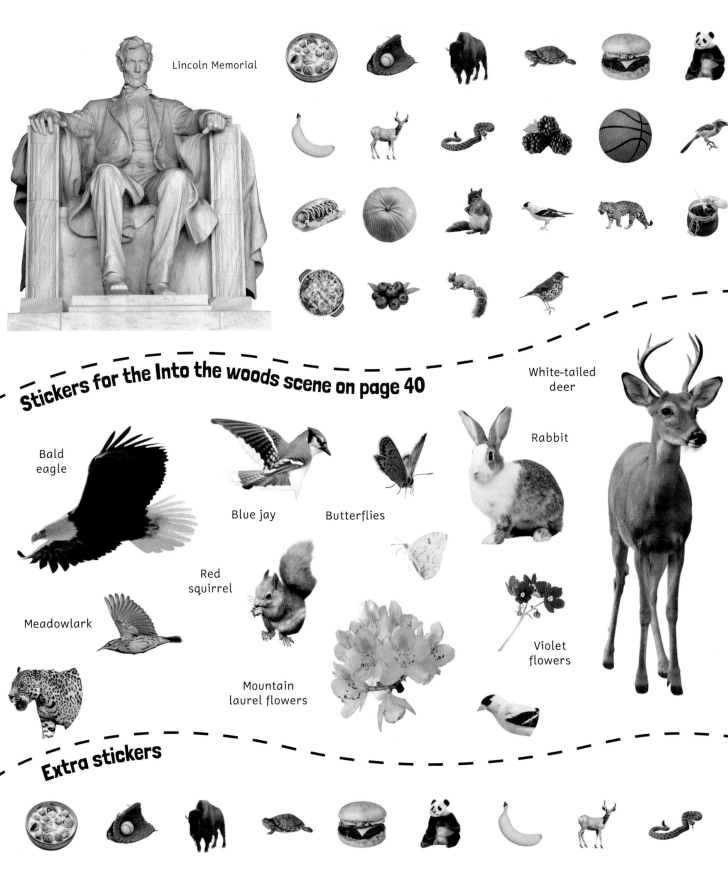

Lincoln Memorial

Stickers for the Into the woods scene on page 40

White-tailed
deer

Rabbit

Bald
eagle

Blue jay

Butterflies

Red
squirrel

Meadowlark

Mountain
laurel flowers

Violet
flowers

Extra stickers